TAUNTON
PAST & PRESENT

Top end of Station Road and Flook House wall, *c.* 1903. The Council had, on previous occasions in 1896 and 1901, tried to buy the land necessary for widening Station Road. Agreement was finally achieved in 1907 when Hanbury and Cotching, the owners of the George Inn, accepted £2,500 for part of the site. A further £1,300 was paid for a strip of land belonging to the owners of Flook House.

The broad expanse of the modern Station Road. The trees surround the town swimming-pool, built in the grounds of Flook House.

TAUNTON
PAST & PRESENT

NICK CHIPCHASE

SUTTON PUBLISHING

First published in the United Kingdom in 2000 by
Sutton Publishing Limited · Phoenix Mill
Thrupp · Stroud · Gloucestershire · GL5 2BU

British Library Cataloguing in Publication Data
A catalogue record for this book is available from the British Library.

ISBN 0-7509-2661-9

Front endpaper: The Parade and Market House, *c.* 1880. The arcades on each side of the Market House were removed in 1930. In the foreground is the Kinglake memorial erected in 1867 and removed by the Council in 1934 to the dismay of local people. Like many earlier photographs this one is posed in order to provide the photographer with a sharper image.
Back endpaper: The Market House now minus the arcades and with less fanciful stonework around the clock. Part of the Parade improvements included wide pavements and the cycle path together with seating and other street furniture.
Half-title page: Fore Street, *c.* 1914. Lewis and Lewis drapery is at nos. 13 and 14 and the 'Tudor' building at that time housed Halliday's Antique shop which opened in 1909. The handcart stands outside Webber's Antique shop formerly the Crown and Mitre Inn.
Title page: Luckily this section of Fore Street has remained largely unaltered during the previous century and has been pedestrianised as part of the Parade enhancement.

Published in association with WHSmith

Galmington Fields in 1905.

Typeset in 11/14pt Photina.
Typesetting and origination by
Sutton Publishing Limited.
Printed in Great Britain by
The Bath Press, Bath.

Contents

A postcard from F. Chapel and Co. of Bristol, *c.* 1906. The views are of the new library (opened 1904) and the Parade market. These views symbolise the theme of this book, which is one of change. Both subjects are still in existence but no longer serve the function they had at the beginning of the century. The library building has become one of the new theme pubs that are becoming popular in the town. The Parade lost its market in 1929 and now even the gardens and grass have gone as the site has finally succumbed to the pressing requirements of Taunton's traffic flow.

Taunton: An Introduction

It has been a great pleasure for me to compile this new volume of photographs, and to include contemporary views to show how places have changed. The concept is not a new one. George Talbot published a book entitled *Taunton Yesterday and Today* in the 1970s which helped provide the inspiration for my own collection of historic photographs. A friend then gave me three old postcards of Taunton and I was hooked. Back in the early 1970s there were little in the way of official photographic archives. Some local views were held by the Francis Frith collection in the form of the original glass negatives. These have been used to produce the high quality views in various publications and as enlargements in various commercial premises.

George Talbot was one of the first true collectors. He found originals and copied them to exhibition standard. Some 370 of these full plate enlargements were given by the Talbot family to the Local Studies Library where they can be seen by the public. Sadly none of the original photographs used by George Talbot can now be traced.

Change is driven by many forces. Some for good and some perhaps not so. Society moves continually onwards. Fashions change. Architecture, transport, shops and technology seldom remain the same for long. Statistics show the massive changes experienced in England since 1900. Male life expectancy at the beginning of the 1900s was 45 (now 74) and the population has almost doubled from 38 million to nearly 60 million. School leaving age has steadily increased from12 years in 1900 and many early views show young children at work pushing handcarts or making deliveries. People in the average home numbered between four and six, now this figure has reduced by nearly half. The motorcar was a rarity in 1900 and there are now over 20 million on the road. The pressure to accommodate this massive increase has shaped our towns and cities more than any other factor.

The public house in the early 1900s was really an extension of our own front rooms. Somewhere warm and cosy where people could chat to friends and perhaps escape from the harsh reality of life. Now is the era of the big theme pub. These and fast food establishments are the growth areas of the late twentieth century. Taunton's tally of public houses reached over 80 in 1903; there are now far fewer in number but probably not so much less in terms of square footage. Also in decline numerically are post offices, corner shops, village schools and a host of small businesses which used to service the local community.

George Talbot's views of Taunton in the 1970s show how much the town has changed in the last 30 years. The architecture of the 1960s tried to move away from the traditional styles using newly developed materials. Now these modern buildings appear dull and lack character – the 'Anytown Architecture' of the late twentieth century.

Planners have more recently reverted to traditional styles and materials and the new Laverock Court on the old Classic Cinema site is a fine example. No doubt as the last thirty years have seen many changes so the next few decades will also bring much change. Perhaps in thirty years time the motorcar will not be so dominant in our towns. I hope this book will serve both as a record of the last one hundred years and a representation of Taunton as it entered the new Millennium.

All the modern photographs in this book, unless otherwise specified, were taken in December 1999.

Opening of the addition to Station Road on 31 October 1907. The ceremony was conducted by the Mayor and Corporation. This was an important day for the town as the Park Fountain and North Town School were also officially opened (see page 93).

High Street & the Town Centre

The Parade and Market House in the 1950s. This layout of lawns and gardens is still much preferred by many Tauntonians to the busy traffic roundabout that exists today. The Burmese memorial (1889) in the background was moved in the mid-1990s to form the centre point of the new roundabout. As long as traffic flow remains a problem in the town centre the present arrangement is unlikely to change. However, a less traffic tolerant society may exist in future years and the Parade may yet return to the domain of the pedestrian.

The Parade market in 1925. This was held on Wednesdays and Saturdays and moved to a new site at Jarvis Field in 1929. To the left are the Victoria Rooms built as the New Market in 1821. The smaller building, centre, was the Corn Exchange (demolished 1937) home to Taunton's first cinema, The Picturedrome, which opened in 1910.

By the 1970s all the buildings on the left before the top of North Street have been replaced by modern architecture. The central Parade is now no longer the province of the pedestrian but serves as a very busy intersection for the town's traffic.

The Burmese memorial in its original position, c. 1925. To the left is part of the Market House arcade. Timothy Whites the popular chemists (later taken over by Boots Ltd) can be seen on the right. The tramway standards had been converted to carry electric lights. The system closed in 1921.

The Burmese memorial, just visible in its new location at the centre of the Parade. The removal of the Market House arcade has opened up the view considerably.

The Parade and North Street, *c.* 1914. A single decker tram emerges from behind the Kinglake memorial. Originally the tramway system comprised of six double decker vehicles when it opened in 1901. In 1905 the tramlines were re-laid and when the system was reopened the single deckers replaced the former type. The Castle Hotel portico can be seen on the left. The roof of this was a convenient position for visiting dignitaries and politicians to address the public.

A similar view taken from a little further back in 1999 to include the Burmese memorial. The arrows point in the direction of traffic flow, which on many occasions is very busy.

An unusual view of the Parade, *c.* 1908. This postcard was commissioned by Hammett and Co., stationers who obviously wished their premises to be in a prominent position on the photograph. Next door to Hammetts is the Devon and Cornwall Bank followed by Boots the Chemists, the last property in North Street. The tall building is Fox, Fowler and Co's bank at no. 32 Fore Street. In the centre is a tramway standard. This carried the 500 volt DC supply which operated the tramcars.

Today's view shows some of the benefits of the recent enhancement of the Parade area. These include wider pavements, a cycle lane, flower tubs and trees.

A view of Hammett Street, *c.* 1905. This street, traditionally the home of the legal and financial professions, was constructed in 1788. On the right is Peark's Stores at 33A Fore Street which in later years became the Maypole Diary Co. (see *Taunton in Old Photographs*, page 42). The tower of St Mary's church is not the original having been completely rebuilt between 1858 and 1860.

The modern Hammett Street which is now one-way as far as the traffic is concerned. Lloyds Bank on the left replaced the buildings occupied by Boots the Chemists and WH Smith. Boots occupied the new building for a while before moving to the High Street.

Buses on the Parade, *c.* 1929. A thirty-two seat National Leyland Lion YC 5228 posted for Pitminster via Trull. The double decker is a Dennis owned by Dunns Motors. The Victoria Rooms are in the background.

Today's new generation of public transport, the 'Shuttle Buses'. In the background the characterless 1960s buildings that replaced the Victoria Rooms.

Fore Street and entrance to Hammett Street, *c.* 1864. An early view before the bank building (now demolished) was constructed on the corner of Hammett Street. The posts and chains surround the Parade.

Today's view showing the Lloyds Bank building. The cobblestones were part of the Parade enhancement scheme.

Fore Street and the Burmese monument, *c.* 1914. The imposing building, left, is the County Club House built by the West of England Banking Co. for their Taunton branch at great cost. The front was constructed of Ham Hill and Lydeard stone relieved by pillars of Aberdeen granite. The motorcar is a 10/12 hp Belsize two seater with dickie seat to fold. The car was dark blue and registered to Florence Woodhouse of Heatherton Park in December 1912.

Woolworth's made a welcome return to the town in April 1998 after an absence of about twenty years. The previous site for the store was at 18A East Street next door to Morelli's Ice Cream Parlour. The new store occupies the former Marks & Spencer premises.

High Street and part of Fore Street, *c.* 1915. The Devon and Somerset Stores are on the left while the buildings on the extreme right form part of the continuation of Fore Street. Woollatt's Chemists moved from 17 Fore Street to 20 Fore Street in 1878 and continued in business until 1906.

No. 20 Fore Street remained a chemists shop (J. Boyds) until it closed in 1979. The premises are now occupied by Thomas Cook who have retained the original door and mosaic floor bearing Woollatt's name. When the chemist shop was converted, the cellar was found to contain many items dating to Woollatt's occupancy including advertisements, toothpaste and cream pots and the delivery boy's cap.

The top end of the High Street, *c.* 1905. This is in the days before pedestrianisation. The three shops on the left are Eastments furniture dealers, Dickenson's bakery at no. 42 and William Nash's greengrocery in the centre with the blind.

The modern High Street is no longer a thoroughfare for traffic. This is surely one of the better planning ideas of recent years.

Upper High Street and entrance to the Crescent pictured just before the street was widened, *c.* 1960. The buildings on the right were demolished. These contained the Somerset County Planning Department, the Fire Brigade HQ and the County Valuers Department. The sign on the wall is advertising Premium Bonds.

All the properties on the north side of Shuttern and Upper High Street have been removed in the last sixty years. This has provided a more spacious route for traffic but problems still occur during rush hours. Just beyond the car is Shuttern Post Office. In the early 1900s the post office was situated in the terrace just past the police station.

East Street & Beyond

Stephen Street, *c* 1906. The street was built around 1900 as part of the Priory Estate development, which included St Augustine Street, Winchester Street, Gyffarde Street and Laburnam Street. Stephen Street consisted of thirty-four houses, several of which were still awaiting completion in 1903. This postcard is from an extensive series by J. Brice, which included many residential back streets.

East Street, *c.* 1925. The tramlines were removed in the early 1920s and there is a mix of traffic on the street. On the right can be seen Montague Coopers Daylight and Electric Photograph Studio at Acacia House. The shop blinds were supported by poles that sat in little cups in the kerbstone.

East Street today with County Walk on the extreme left. To the right the large building recently vacated by the Co-op and converted to a Primark store early in 2000.

East Street and County Hotel 1925. At the turn of the century, it was known as the London Hotel. It dates back to 1528 when it was called the Three Cups, and is the oldest recorded public house in Taunton. Trust Houses Ltd bought the London Hotel in 1919 and renamed it the County Hotel (see also page 55).

The County Hotel building now occupied by Waterstones Book shop and Marks & Spencer.

Paul Street looking north towards East Street, *c.* 1890. Now extensively redeveloped, the street contained four pubs at the turn of the century – the Prince of Wales, the King and Queen Inn, the Boot Inn and the Devonshire Inn.

Hardly recognisable today, Paul Street now no longer gives traffic access to East Street. Half way down on the left is the town library and access to the multi storey car parks.

East Street, *c.* 1939. Many of the buildings in the view have been redeveloped although that of the Phoenix Hotel remains the same. The clock is on the Cooperative Society Stores looking as much out of place in the 1930s as it does today. The motor car BYB 90 is a 8 hp Ford registered in 1936.

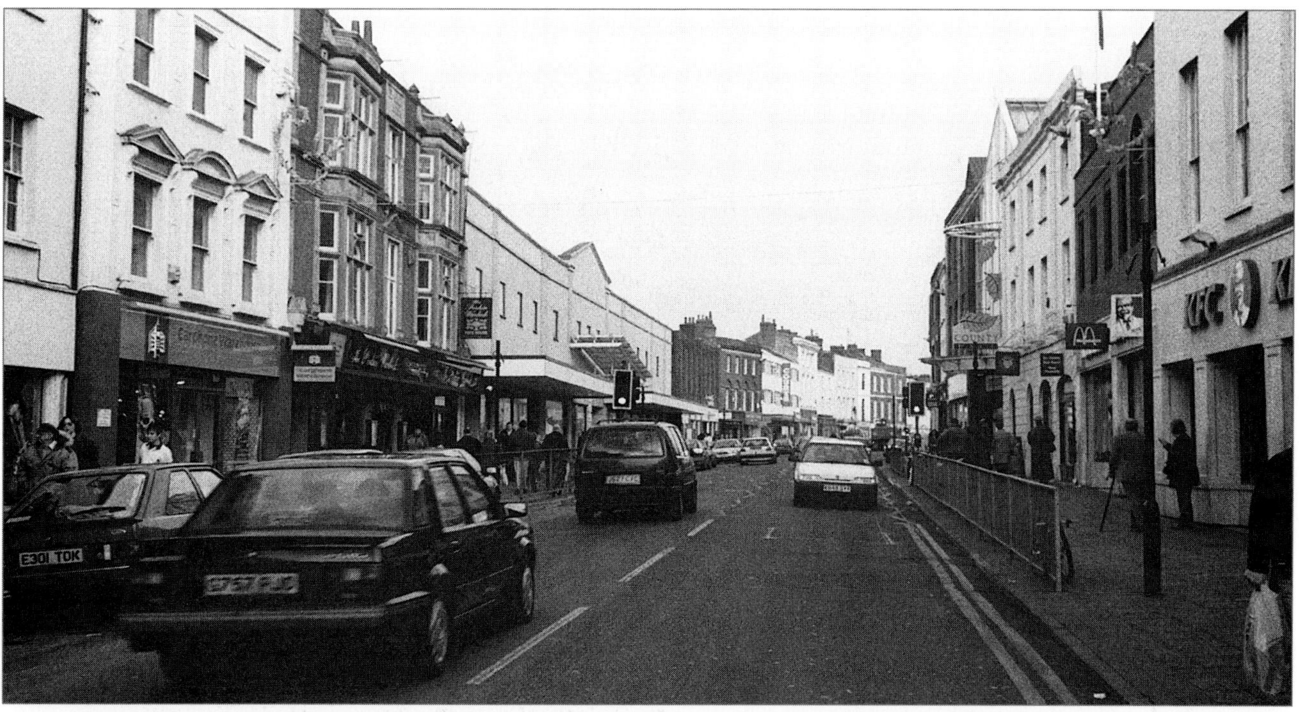

The Co-op building having swallowed up adjoining properties now squats like a giant monolith in East Street. Brave, forward looking architecture in the 1950s and 1960s but sadly amiss today. Primark moved from the High Street in April 2000 to re-open in the former Co-op.

East Street and East Gate, *c.* 1890. Pope's almshouses (founded 1590), on the left, housed nine poor women, spinsters or widows of good character. These were demolished in 1933, the site becoming Dunn's Motors at nos. 43–5 East Street. Near the centre is the pump, which formed part of the public water supply. Gray's Almshouses on the right were established in 1635 and are possibly the oldest surviving brick built houses in the town.

The boisterous Chicago Rock Café and Gray's Almshouses for those seeking a quiet retirement seem unlikely neighbours in today's East Street.

Old shops in East Street, *c.* 1890. This view is an enlargement from the original glass negative used on the previous page. The doorway between H.J. Rowe, fruiterer and A.W. Lee, hairdresser led into one of the many Courts of Taunton, often poor quality accommodation where many townspeople lived.

Chicago Rock Café, one of several theme pubs now gaining popularity in the town. A new and modern concept but still managing some refinement in outward appearances.

East Reach, *c.* 1904. The granite drinking fountain in the foreground now resides in Vivary Park. The author has two childhood memories related to this junction – one is the underground toilets, which may still remain intact below the road. Poole's Refreshment Rooms became the Rainbow Café an ideal spot for escaping Askwith School in nearby South Street.

Locals christened East Reach 'Disco Drive' when all the traffic lights sprang up. Like most main streets, it is horrendously busy in the rush hours. It's a pity the trees are no longer there.

East Reach and the Taunton and Somerset Hospital, *c.* 1910. The hospital foundation stone was laid in 1810 and it opened for business on 25 March 1812. The building was greatly enlarged in 1841 when the east and west wings were added at a cost of £3,000. Further enlargements took place in the 1870s and the Victoria Nursing Institute was added next door. The hospital is now closed, all departments having been transferred to Musgrove.

The old hospital building and Nursing Institute have been refurbished and contain offices. The Institute building is appropriately named Nightingale House.

East Reach nos. 145, 146 and 147, *c.* 1910. W.H. Knight and Son were organ builders at no. 145, later becoming music sellers and, by the 1930s, musical instrument dealers. J. Wadden (centre) was a manufacturers of ropes, nets and cart covers trading from this address for a short while before moving on to 154 East Reach by 1914 (later no.137). No. 147 appears to have been a private residence with the Albion Inn next door up.

No. 146 East Reach had been redeveloped to become Dibben's Builders Merchants in the 1960s. Later this business became the Devon Trading Co. Taunton Tile and Bathroom Centre now occupies the premises while a dazzling display of light fittings can be seen at no. 145.

Single decker tram near the depot at the end of East Reach, *c.* 1905. This view was obviously photographed quite soon after the introduction of these trams, as the car is not yet carrying advertising placards. Beyond this point the track took a long curve into the depot just beyond Alfred Street (now Victoria Parkway). The wall behind surrounded Leycroft House garden.

With the construction of Victoria Parkway this area became one of the busiest road junctions in Taunton (also incorporating the tallest lampstand in the town surmounted by CCTV camera).

Silver Street and the beginning of South Road, *c.* 1909. In 1903 these houses were home to a watchmaker and a sanitary inspector, together with other private individuals.

Silver Street now not quite as neat and uniform as in the earlier view. All the little gardens and iron railings have long since disappeared.

North Street & Beyond

North Street, *c.* 1910. On the left hand side is the frontage of the Castle Hotel before it amalgamated with Clarke's Hotel on Castle Green. Barter and Duder (right), established in 1836, became County Stores. Westminster House next door was rebuilt before the 1920s.

North Street, late 1920s. W.H. Smith's store on the right collapsed dramatically overnight in 1959 (see *Taunton Revisited*, page 90). Motor traffic has now superseded the horse drawn vehicles. The car parked next to the disused tramway standard is an Austin, registered to the Taunton Motor Co. in 1927. Chapman's department store, now Debenhams, can be seen at the bottom of the street.

Today's North Street with Principles store, formally Burtons, on the left. The Burtons store was built in 1929 after the amalgamation of Clarkes and the Castle Hotel.

North Street, *c.* 1914. A.E. de Breffe and Co.'s antique shop is at no. 48 occupying the former Nags Head Hotel from 1912. W.H. Maunder's chemist shop, previously the business of A.J. Smith, is next door. Percy Pearce's tailoring business is now Barclays Bank. This relatively quiet view was sold as a postcard by Bakers Stationary shop in Bridge Street.

Today's North Street now one of the busiest shopping streets in Taunton. The street has changed considerably in the last 100 years. In 1903 there were two chemist's, six public houses and hotels, and a host of smaller shops. Today the larger multiple stores and banks have prominence.

North Street and the GPO building, *c.* 1932. The post office opened in 1911 having been built by Pollard and Son of Bridgwater at a cost of £7,000. The first shop with the blind was owned by Mac Fisheries Ltd. The car outside the GPO is a Clyno 10.8 hp registered to R.B Gibson of Taunton in March 1927. This model, introduced in 1922 was the company's first successful motorcar. Other models were marketed but the company collapsed in 1929.

North Street with Christmas decorations, 1999. The GPO remains the same but British Home Stores' modern premises have replaced the prominent building at nos. 40 and 41 next to the former Mac Fisheries.

Corner of St James Street and top of Bridge Street, *c.* 1860. The bridge is on the extreme left with Bridge House just evident.

St James Street became one way to traffic some years ago. The Jessops building bears the date 1892. Originally these buildings were numbered as 'The Bridge' but they now form part of Bridge Street which itself has been renumbered.

The old stone arch bridge, *c.* 1893. The old bridge was partially reconstructed in 1834 and when no longer adequate to the town's needs, was replaced in 1894. Bridge House, visible in this view, is now obscured by the Dellars building. The view was published on a postcard from an original illustration by Charles Colman.

The modern town bridge was built in 1894 at a cost of £7,000. The bridge is actually shorter now than it was in 1894. Land reclamation and new buildings were subsequently added on the north side. The prominent building on the right is the site of the old Dellars Café now a nightclub.

The south side of the bridge, *c.* 1950. Webbers Sports occupied the corner block at this time – adjoining stores are Bartletts ladies hairdressers, Redstones Drapery, Gillards Tobacconists, Elise Costumiers, Fayes Jewellers and Percy Taylor electrical and radio engineer on the corner of St James Street.

The buildings have not changed much in the last 50 years. All the shops are now different, however, except for one – the sewing machine shop on the extreme right. The bridge survived severe flooding in 1960 when masses of timber from the nearby timberyard became jammed underneath.

Bridge Street from the bridge, *c.* 1911. The *County Herald* offices are on the left. The poster outside advertises the popular Taunton Dog Show, which was cancelled during the First World War and restarted again in 1921 after a seven year break.

Bridge Street in 1999. The block on the left, formerly Allen's Garage, has been redeveloped to include a number of smaller shops. Beyond this is the entrance to Wood Street, which was widened by the demolition of the Labour Exchange.

Bridge Street at the time of Queen Victoria's 1897 Diamond Jubilee. The building on the left is North Town Grocery and Provision Stores. Next door is the Telegraph Inn before the building was reconstructed around 1900.

Bridge Street, 1999. From here a run of charity shops now extend down into Station Road. The Telegraph Inn has been renamed the Cider Press. The town's association with cider production is far less evident today than it was in the past with the recent closure of Taunton Cider at Norton Fitzwarren.

Station Road, *c.* 1903. The children are probably waiting for Sanger's Circus procession to Jarvis Field (now the market). At this time the street was quite narrow, it was widened in 1907 with the demolition of the George Inn and the wall surrounding Flook House.

Today a garage occupies part of the site on the west side. To the immediate left is scaffolding surrounding the new flats that have been built on the old Classic Cinema site (Laverock Court).

Station Road looking towards the station, *c.* 1914. The properties on the left have long since lost their gardens. Just beyond the gardens is Westlake's Cycle Depot with the blind at no. 49. This picture offers a good view of the tramway passing loop in Station Road which was one of nine on the system.

Today's Station Road. The junction with Belvedere Road is on the left. All the former private houses on the left have been converted to shops.

Station Road, *c.* 1910. The junction with Albermarle Road is on the left. Tom Male's Grocery shop between the Royal Mail Stores and the Crown and Sceptre was removed to create access into Priory Bridge Road. At this time there was only a narrow entrance into Canal Road.

It is odd how we have become used to traffic directions in the road. They really only become apparent when compared to earlier views. The need to maintain increasing traffic flows have had a major influence on the appearance and development of the town in the last fifty years.

A Holt tractor draws an eight-inch howitzer into Station Approach. These American built agricultural tractors proved to be ideal for moving heavy artillery. This vehicle has the name 'The Flying Dutchman', painted on the radiator. The heavy gun was a typical piece of British ingenuity. Six-inch naval guns from store were rebored to eight inches and mounted on traction engine wheels. At some point it was decided to incorporate the whole arrangement into one unit and this led directly to the development of the tank. The bridge carries the loop of railway track that runs around and avoids Taunton Station.

The large house between the two railway bridges no longer exists. Much of the overgrown garden remains a tiny natural reserve within an urban area.

Maxwell Street, Rowbarton, *c.* 1905. The street consisted of 32 houses and a shop at no. 27 in 1903. The local children have appeared for photographer Mr E. Cox.

Now no children but plenty of cars in Maxwell Street. Many of the houses in this area originally housed employees of the Great Western Railway.

Leslie Avenue photographed around 1906. The street is not listed in the town directory of 1903 so the buildings in the photograph had only recently been built. On the opposite side of the street is Rowbarton Recreation Ground.

The house on the corner has been converted into a shop. At the beginning of the century there were about seventy of these little shops serving the local community. Now perhaps less than a quarter of them survive.

Waverley Terrace off Richmond Road, *c.* 1906. The lamp near the end of the terrace marks the Frieze Hill Inn at nos. 5 and 6. This photograph was produced as a postcard by Henry Montague Cooper of East Street.

The same terrace today. The public house no longer exists, having reverted to two private houses. As in many views, the original ironwork has been replaced by a brick wall. Presumably the railings were removed in the late 1940s to aid the war effort.

Pubs & Hotels

Visit of the Cork Club to the Railway Inn at Norton Fitzwarren 1926. The photo shows a mixture of locals and members of the club. The Cork Club visited local public houses (in this case by charabanc) to sample the ales and cider on offer. The pub building is now owned by Matthew Clark Ltd the proprietors of Taunton Cider. The building may be demolished if the extensive redevelopment planned for Norton takes place.

The Castle Hotel, *c.* 1930. The property was built in 1815 as a private house for the Easton family and was converted to a hotel in 1834. The building was erected close to the line of the outer moat surrounding Taunton Castle and incorporated the ruined Castle Eastgate. The foundations of the Castle Keep were excavated in the garden of the hotel 1924–29.

Clarkes Hotel and the Castle Hotel were two separate businesses amalgamated in 1928 by Harrison's Hotels Limited who owned both premises. The original Clarkes had two stories but a third was added in the 1920s. The fourth storey came in 1965 and the famous wisteria, dating back to at least 1900, now covers the entire frontage.

The Half Moon Inn (left) and Spread Eagle Inn (far right), North Street, *c.* 1893. Between the two pubs are Bond's Pure Sweet Shop with entrance to Half Moon Court below and then Scott's Coventry House at no. 38 North Street was a jewellers.

The old Half Moon Inn building still bears Starkey, Knight and Ford's trademark flying horse. The Spread Eagle was demolished to make way for the new post office building.

The Dolphin Inn, Duke Street, *c.* 1920. The bar ran from Duke Street through to King Street with a ballroom above. After the building was demolished a new Dolphin Inn was built at Holway but this has recently been renamed the Flying Horse. The new name presumably arises from Starkey, Knight and Fords trademark on the wall of the pub.

The north side of Duke Street originally consisted of Paradise Square, the Dolphin Inn then nos. 1–12 Tone Cottages. King Street then ran parallel to Duke Street. The whole area has now been redeveloped and converted to flats.

The Kings Arms, Staplegrove Road, *c.* 1900. The Inn was rebuilt around 1910. In the 1950s the pub car park was an important staging post for local buses and coaches.

The modern Kings Arms Inn. The building has been much enlarged and is one of the few pubs in Taunton to have skittle alleys.

The Three Mariners Inn, High Street, decorated for the Coronation of George VI, 1937. This pub was right next door to the Green Dragon. During the 1950s the building housed the Three Mariners Snack Bar.

This section of the High Street has been completely rebuilt. Darlows Estate Agent now occupies the site.

County Hotel, 1925. From 1910 until 1934 a cinema was housed in the former Assembly Rooms behind the hotel and cinema placards appear in many 1920s photographs. The former cinema became the Empire Hall and this was the venue for many functions and meetings after the war including an election speech by Winston Churchill in 1950. Following renovation the Empire Hall and ballroom emerged as the County Ballroom in 1960.

The County Hotel closed in the mid-1990s and the building was redeveloped for shops, of which Waterstone's bookshop is the largest. Marks & Spencer also moved and its old store in East Street was taken over by Woolworth's.

Ashton Temperance Hotel, *c.* 1910. The Temperance movement was strongly represented in Taunton in the early 1900s. There were thirteen Temperance societies in the town in 1903 and five Temperance Hotels. The directory for that year stated that 'Temperance Hotels have become essential factors in the commercial arrangement of a town'. The business at the Ashton was established in 1869 by Mrs Grace Ashton.

In 1910 the hotel comprised of writing and smoke rooms, ladies drawing and private sitting rooms together with twenty well appointed bedrooms. Today the hotel is of similar outward appearance but it has been many years since it was last a Temperance establishment.

Four All's Hotel, *c.* 1950. The original building was situated in Tower Street adjoining old cottages. The hotel was reconstructed sometime after 1894 when Corporation Street was built. Plans produced in 1948 for a major road through Bath Place to the Parade would have resulted in the demolition of the building and the whole of Bath Place. Luckily the plans were shelved.

The Four Alls Hotel is now known as the Voodoo Lounge. The old Somerset Motors site on the left has been redeveloped to become Michael Paul House.

Phoenix Hotel from *A Plan for Taunton* published in 1948. The photograph also shows W.P. Edwards' shop, formerly the Taunton Cycle Works (see page 89). Eastman's family butchers had been on this site since the early 1900s.

The Phoenix Hotel building has survived redevelopment and now houses a restaurant and dry cleaners. Two icons of the modern age, McDonald's and Kentucky Fried Chicken, are next door.

Tom Marchant's Shakespeare Inn (with clock) and the Racehorse Inn, East Reach, *c.* 1959. Possibly the Shakespeare Inn's name originated from the fact that Taunton's first permanent theatre opened behind here in 1786.

The Shakespeare Inn was demolished around 1960 and now White Bros. frontage extends right up to the Racehorse.

The George Hotel, High Street, *c.* 1970. In this view the former Devon and Somerset Stores site is still awaiting development. The hotel building was itself rebuilt but the outer façade was left intact. The hotel possibly dated back to the early seventeenth century.

Now of course the High Street is pedestrianised and the George Hotel has closed to become Country Casuals. The former Perkins butchers shop now sells discs and tapes.

Buildings

One of Taunton's most prominent buildings, the former Leper Hospital, *c.* 1905. Although a leper colony existed on the site in the twelfth century the present building dates to around 1515 and a small leper colony still existed here in 1548. By the early seventeenth century the building had become a poor house for West Monkton and was often referred to as Spitalfields Almshouse, a corrupted form of the word hospital.

The Leper Hospital, *c.* 1890. The Alms House closed in 1938 and the building became the home of the Somerset Guild of Craftsmen. The building occupied by H. Browning, butcher, (and later by W.P. Edwards) was possibly a former chapel and was demolished around 1930.

The sorry state of St Margaret's Leper Hospital in 1999. After two arson attacks the building is boarded up and covered with a sheet. Recently a £130,000 rescue deal was announced to turn the dilapidated premises back into almshouses, which should open by the year 2001.

The Gaumont Cinema, Corporation Street, *c.* 1933. The cinema was built by Albany Ward Theatres in 1932 on land sold by the Council for £14,000 and later renamed the Odeon. Included in the proposals was a new road through to Tower Street now called Castle Way.

The cinema was closed by the proprietors in 1981 and the premises converted to Top Rank Bingo. Apparently this was considered to be a better use of the building's large seating capacity. The building on the extreme right was built as a technical institute and opened by Mayor W.A. Wrenn in 1900. It originally contained classrooms and laboratories for electrical, physical and mechanical work.

The Lyceum Cinema, *c.* 1920. The cinema opened on 18 August 1913 with the showing of the silent classic *Quo Vadis*. It had been built on the site of the former George Inn. The posters are advertising *Broadway Rose* and *The Way of the Eagle*.

The Lyceum became the Odeon and later the Classic Cinema before it was finally demolished in 1998. At the end of 1999 a new prestigious block of flats was nearing completion. This became Laverock Court in 2000 named after Les Laverock, the former manager of the cinema.

St Andrews Church, Rowbarton, *c.* 1890. The church was built in 1880 by H.J. Spiller at a cost of £2,500 and dedicated in 1883.

In 1893 St Andrews was enlarged by the addition of a wide south aisle, a morning chapel and a western lobby. The chancel was also lengthened by 12 feet.

Trinity Church and Schools, *c.* 1860. The Ecclesiastical Parish of Trinity was formed out of St Mary's in 1842 and the church was built by subscription in the same year. The school buildings were erected at his own cost by the first incumbent Reverend F.J. Smith.

Around the late 1960s the school was demolished and moved to the former Askwith School in South Street. Blocks of flats now occupy the site.

The Victoria Rooms on the Parade, *c.* 1918. This was built as the New Market in 1821 and was later known as the Victoria Rooms and then the Town Hall. The premises housed the fruit and vegetable side of the market and contained the British Restaurant during the Second World War. The building was demolished in 1963.

Unfortunately the Victoria Rooms were replaced by 'Anytown Architecture', buildings of little character which can be seen in most towns in England. The Parade enhancement has at least brought some trees back into the scene.

Somerset Constabulary Headquarters, *c.* 1940. The building originally formed part of Wilton prison which closed in 1884. In 1940 the premises also housed the Motor Taxation Department and the County Weights and Measures Office. The town police station was across the road. This was built in 1856 and demolished in 1963. The ground floor windows have been sandbagged to protect them from bomb damage.

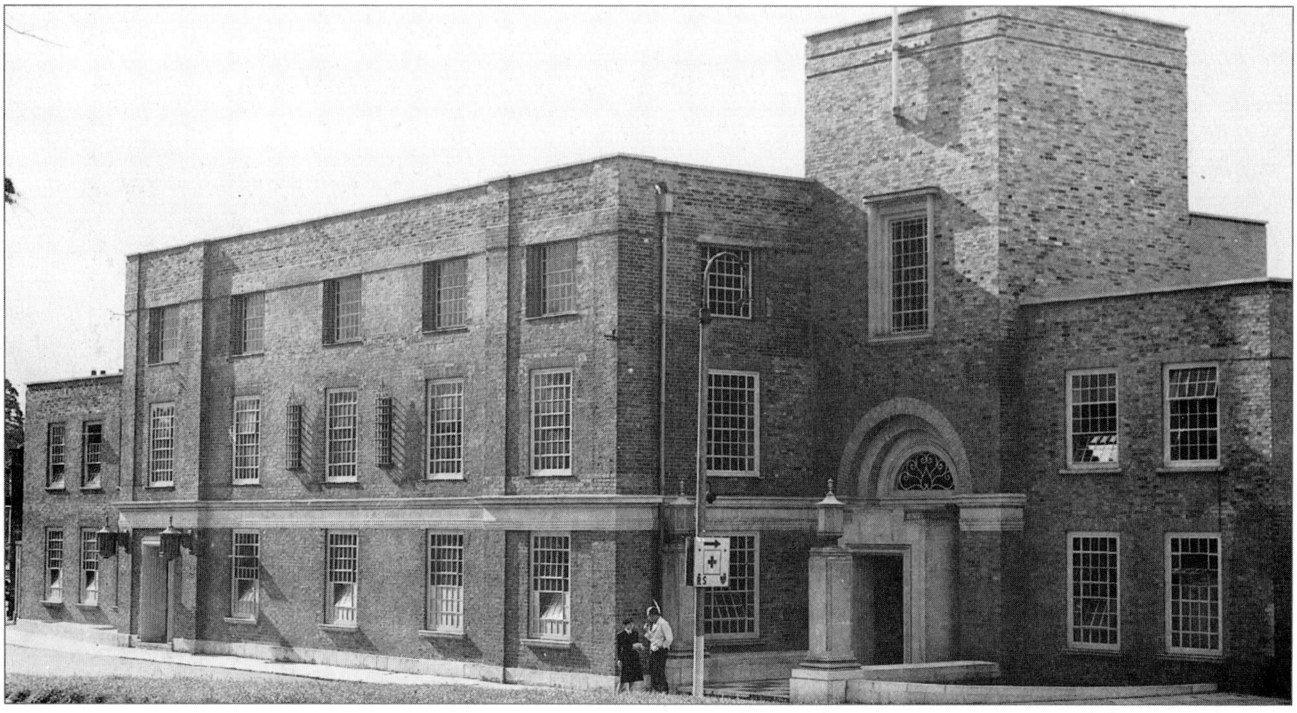

In 1943 the Constabulary Headquarters was reconstructed. The building now houses Taunton Police Station.

Jellalabad Barracks, *c.* 1907. The barracks were completed in 1880 and were the home of the Somerset Light Infantry. Originally the Somerset Regiment, the name was changed to Prince Albert's Regiment of Light Infantry in 1842. The S.L.I saw service in Burma and Afghanistan and the barracks were named after one of their triumphs. The Regiment merged with the Duke of Cornwall's Light Infantry in 1959 and, after housing the Army Pay Corps for a while, the barracks eventually closed.

Apart from the prominent keep most of the barracks have been demolished. The redevelopment site including the parade ground is now private housing, parking areas and gardens.

Rowbarton Congregational Chapel, c. 1910. The chapel was originally built in 1869 and then reconstructed in 1910. The building was demolished in 1972.

The site of the former Rowbarton Congregational Chapel. The stone on the left marks the chapel's demolition.

The Municipal Buildings and rear entrance to Victoria Rooms market, *c.* 1904. The Municipal Buildings were originally built as a grammar school in 1522 by Bishop Richard Fox. This view would have been the rear of the school, Corporation Street having been constructed through the gardens, originally the castle moat, in 1893–94. The stone wall and steps were built along higher ground, the former earthwork defences of the castle.

The Municipal Buildings remain unchanged but the ornate rear entrance to the Victoria Rooms has been replaced by a fairly unexciting modern building.

Weirfield School, *c.* 1905. The school was started in 1879 by J.G. Loveday, a master at Taunton School. Mrs Janet Loveday was the principal. The school was originally designed to educate the sisters of boys at Taunton School.

Weirfield Green, the former site of Weirfield School. The school buildings have been demolished and the seven acres of grounds are now a housing estate.

The corner of Corporation Street and the Parade, *c.* 1902. The tall building housed Stuckey's Banking Co. with Lipton's shop on the left. The building on the right is one of the Market House arcades demolished in 1930.

Sometime before 1923 the rather fine bank building was demolished together with Liptons shop. Much of the elegant architecture surrounding the Parade has been demolished and replaced by very ordinary buildings with little character or style. Some modern guidebooks are critical of Taunton's architecture. In the last seventy years we have lost the Victoria Rooms, the bank building on the corner of Hammett Street, the County Club, the Corn Exchange, the Devon and Somerset Stores and the Market House arcades. The Kinglake memorial has also been removed.

Old shops in East Reach, *c.* 1951. The centre shop is the Cassana Cake Co. Bakery at no. 119. These buildings were demolished to make way for the Octagon Chapel.

The building on the far left still remains and now houses a Cantonese Restaurant (with suitable oriental modifications to the frontage). The Octagon Chapel, which opened in 1965, is set back from the road. The old chapel in Middle Street was converted to the Camelot Nightclub.

Bishop Fox's School, Staplegrove Road, *c.* 1910. This view shows the rear of the building and the girls' playground. The school originally opened in the Crescent in 1890 and these new buildings were erected in 1904 and enlarged in 1907. The school moved to Kingston Road in 1940.

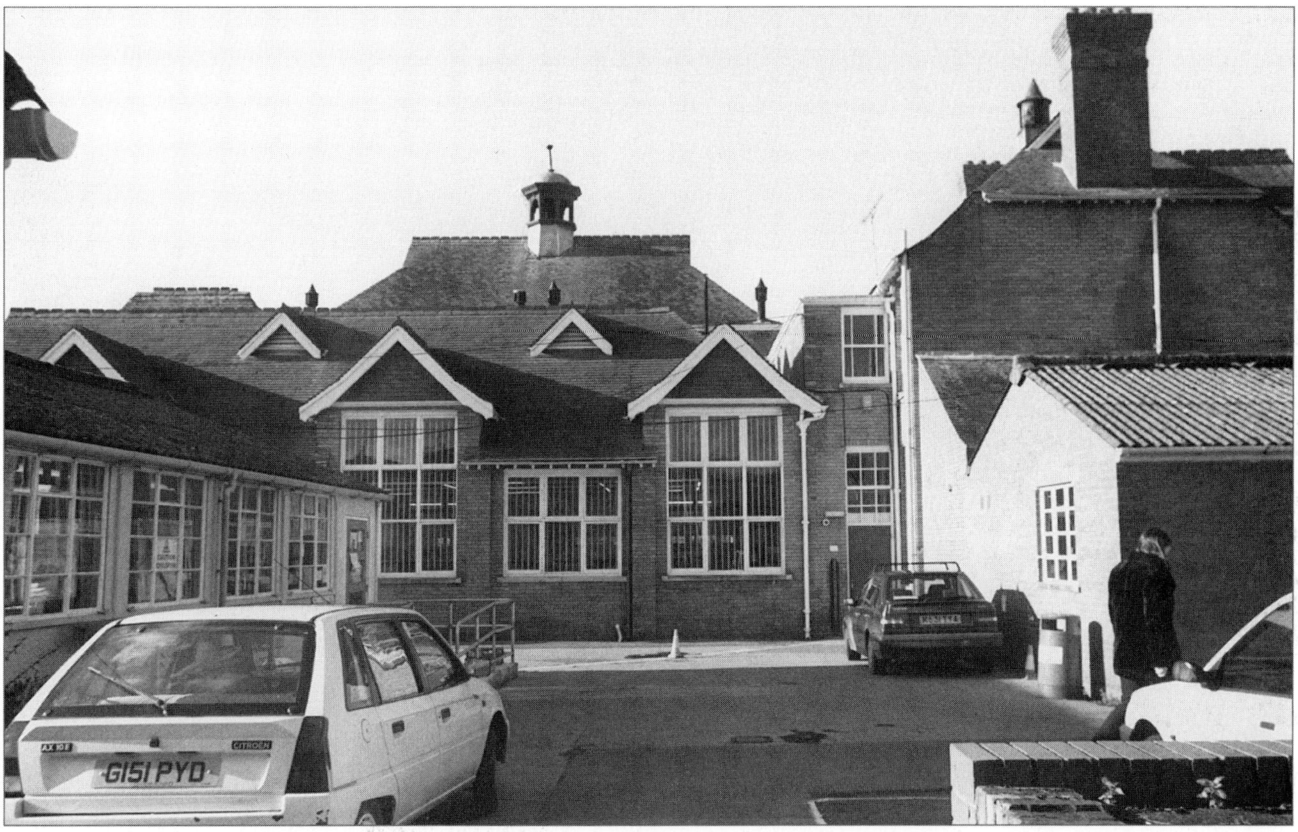

Now a branch of the Somerset Collage for Arts and Technology, the former school playground is covered by temporary buildings.

Huish's School East Street, *c.* 1907. Originally housed in the old grammar school in Corporation Street, the school moved to the site of the former Green's Commercial School in East Street in 1881. New buildings were completed in 1892 funded by grants from the County Council.

Huish's School moved to new premises in South Road in 1964 and the area was redeveloped to include Sainsbury's Supermarket and a new link road from Silver Street to Billet Field (Hurdle Way). This view shows some of the car park that now exists on part of the school site, with Hurdle Way in the background.

Commerce

Hembrow's Garage no. 74 East Reach, *c.* 1930. Many of the town's garages started in quite a small way, concentrating on hiring and repairs with perhaps one or two pumps for motor spirit. Some, like Whites and Allens, developed into main dealerships while others concentrated on the sale of petrol. The near continuous Edwardian frontages of East Reach have, in the last 50 years, been seriously affected by garage forecourt development.

Frank Bryant's Wine and Spirit Vaults at no. 50 Fore Street, *c.* 1925. This business was started by George Bryant around 1895 and was taken over by Frank Bryant about 25 years later. The business continued until the 1940s. The window poster advertises South African Hock at 2/6d (12½p).

F. Adam's Fruit and Florist shop at no. 59 High Street, *c.* 1900. The archway on the left is part of the Bell Inn. Adam's business was established in 1877 with premises also at nos. 5 and 7 Station Road and 15 North Parade. There were nurseries at North Town.

No. 50 is the last premises in Fore Street before the start of East Street. In the early 1970s Colmer's Department Store occupied the site (nos. 47–50). WH Smith's store now stands on the site.

Today's view shows a part of High Street that has been extensively redeveloped to include major stores and Crown Walk.

Hawkes and Sons, ironmongers and agricultural and horticultural agents, 32 and 33 East Street, *c.* 1905. This display shows a fine range of implements. Hawkes also supplied cake, oil and manure together with laundry and dairy machinery.

Hawkes' premises were demolished and the site investigated by archaeologists in 1977. Occupation appears to date back to the late Saxon times and the area formed part of the town's medieval defences. An Argos store now stands on the site.

Arthur Steevens complete house furnishers at no. 62 East Street, *c.* 1907. John Steevens, a designer and manufacturer of cabinet furniture, established the business in 1836. The firm eventually passed to his son Arthur and the company sold new and antique furniture, beds and carpets, Liberty's art fabrics and ceramics from the major potteries. Extensively altered in 1903, the premises totalled 40,000 square feet of showrooms, workshops and warehousing.

A different type of store (C&A) but on much the same scale as Steeven's premises. Billet Street no longer gives vehicles access to East Street. A shock decision to close all of their stores was announced by C&A in June 2000.

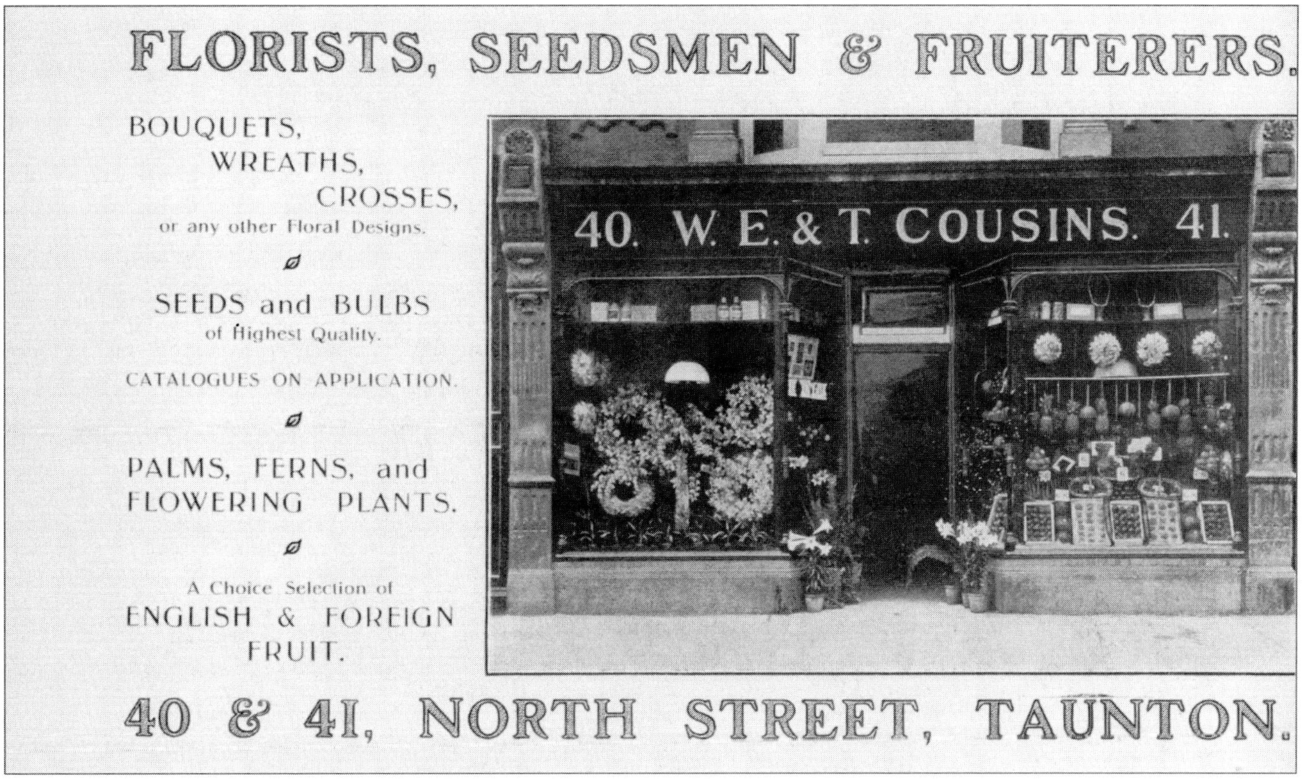

Cousins Florists, seedsmen and fruiterers at nos. 40 and 41 North Street, *c.* 1907. The company moved here from 37 North Street in 1900.

A definite change of style now with British Home Stores occupying the site.

Devon and Somerset Stores pictured just before demolition in 1968. Originally the White Hart Inn, the building was converted to Jacob's General Furnishing Warehouse in 1865. Shortly afterwards the business became the Devon and Somerset Stores with a branch in Exeter. The store advertised itself as cash dealers in over 10,000 articles.

A new shop was erected on the site built in a similar style to the old stores. This currently houses a shoe shop.

Spiller and Webber builders merchants at 7 Bridge Street, *c.* 1925. The business was founded early in 1890 by Charles Webber – who had previously been connected with Colthurst and Co., timber merchants – and George Spiller. The original trade was described as ironmongers, oil, colour and glass merchants. In 1912 the business became a limited company.

A new shop was constructed for Spiller and Webber by J.H. Moggridge and Sons in 1937. The work was done over the course of a year, mostly at night. The fourth floor was added in 1956. In 1985 the company became part of the Stansell's Group. The penny farthing logo was adopted in 1987. The machine was originally owned by Mr Spiller and has now been restored. On 7 April 2000 a new revamped 'Lifestyle' store was opened following major refurbishment.

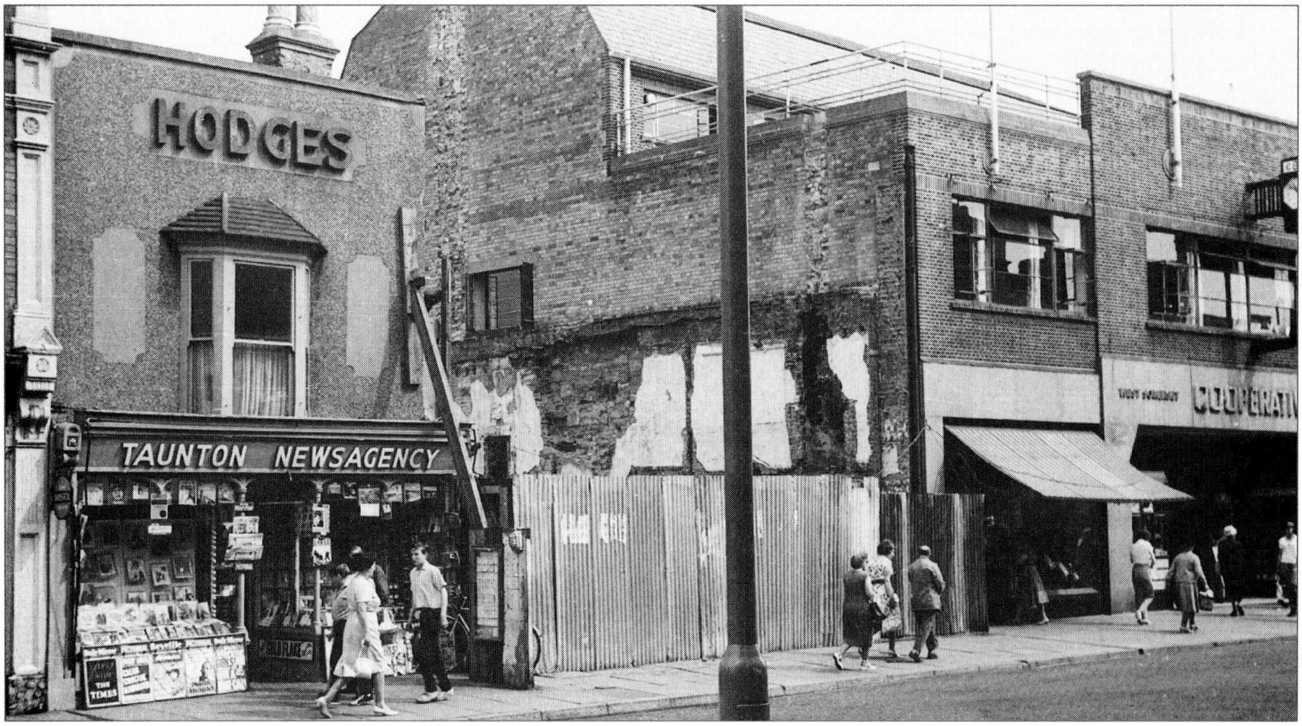

Hodges newsagency and the Co-op Store, *c.* 1963. The umbrella shop and confectioners, which had stood between the two, was demolished to make way for an extension to the Co-op. Eventually the Co-op also took over the Hodges site.

The Co-op store late in 1999 during conversion to a new store for Primark, which opened in April 2000.

Walter Cozens bakers cart at Ruishton, *c.* 1907. The bakers roundsman was a common site in the early 1900s. Most local villages had a bakery and twenty-eight bakers are listed in the Taunton Directory of 1903.

Len Webber's bakers van at Ruishton, *c.* 1960. Not a 1999 view for once but still quite a contrasting scene. Mr Webber was born in 1903 and worked for Norton Mills for over 50 years. By the end of the 1960s bakeries in the town had declined in number to twelve.

H.W. Pring's dairy and shop at the corner of Grays Road, *c.* 1959. There were three small general shops here in 1903.

The same premises, still a shop but retailing fishing tackle and airguns. To the right is one of the several garage forecourts in East Reach that have considerably disrupted the continuous building line of the Edwardian era.

James Pearsall and Co. Ltd Silk Throwsters at East Gate House, *c.* 1960. In the 1780s there were 800 silk looms worked by 1,800 employees in the town. The number of workers had increased to nearly 4,500 by 1820. Partly due to French imports, the industry declined and Pearsall's were the last major manufacturers in the town employing over 200 workers in the 1970s. The building housed Sibley and Thornes drapery in 1905.

After closure, the silk factory was demolished and replaced by this oddly truncated building. The area to the rear has been redeveloped for residential purposes and named Eastgate Gardens.

W.H. Stone's cycle showrooms at 39A Bridge Street, *c.* 1907. Stone's motor garage was in Staplegrove Road. The company offered for sale the largest stock of new and used cycles in the town.

Bridge Street was renumbered around 1950 and the premises now occupy no. 25 which housed Bridge Sports Ltd in the 1970s. In 1999 the site was once again occupied by a cycle shop – the Bike Zone.

Taunton Cycle Works, 58 East Street, *c.* 1905. The proprietor, B.E. Dening, also owned the Taunton Carriage Works. New workshops were opened behind the East Street premises in 1911. Mr C. Webber stands on the left.

W.P. Edwards owned this property in the 1950s. It later became part of the Taunton Motor Co. (Wadham Stringer), and then McDonald's.

W.A. Upham, 3 Shuttern, *c.* 1908. Upham's were ladies and gentleman's tailors offering a 'splendid assortment of rain coatings, suitings, breeches, tweeds, trouserings, livery and habit cloths'. Next door on the right was Chaffer's bakery. The carriage is either a Barouche or Victoria.

Modern 'carriages' outside Louise's hair design salon. The former bakery frontage next door remains relatively unchanged.

Tone Sweet Depot at no. 2 The Bridge, *c.* 1902. The owner of the shop, Miss E.M. Richards, came to a tragic end in February 1903. She lived alone above the shop and was found dead with two empty packets of rat poison close by. The coroner recorded a verdict of suicide while temporarily insane.

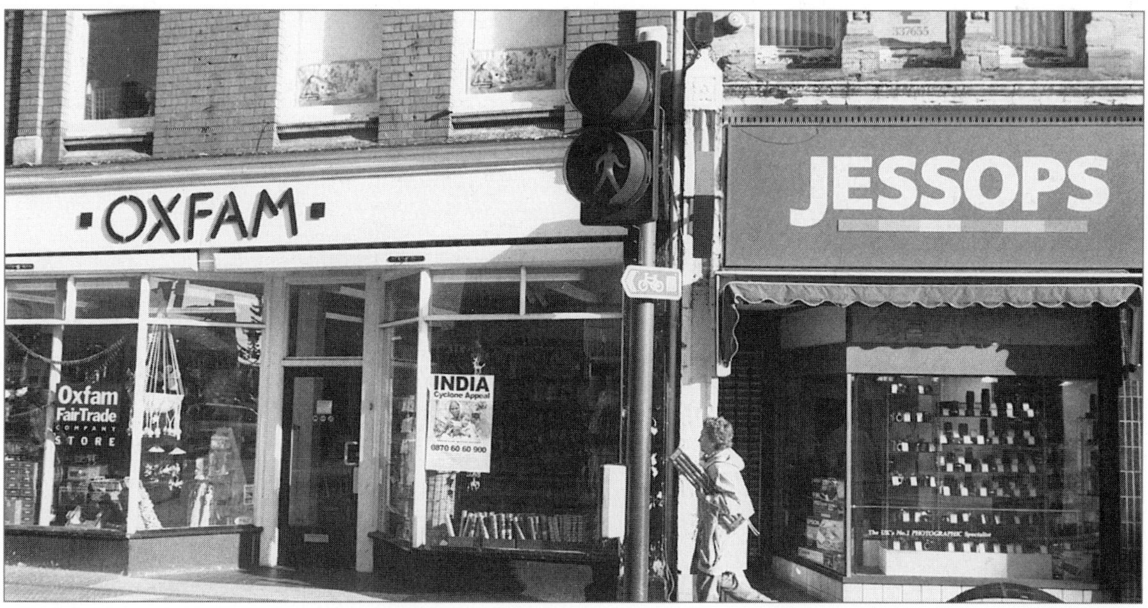

The street numbers have changed in intervening years. The Sweet Depot would have been situated approximately in this position on the bridge.

W. Lock and Co. Wholesale grocers, 12 North Street, *c.* 1905. Another one of those specially commissioned postcards that are so collectable and hard to locate today. With five collections and deliveries a day the postcard was a very cheap and efficient means of communication before the telephone became commonplace. Around 1908 the business became G. West and Son.

The building remains much the same although the fine Edwardian frontage has long since disappeared.

Knapman and Reeves (The Blouse Shop) 17 North Street, *c.* 1920. This business was located here from around 1919 to the mid-1930s. The property then became home to Leslie Giles Opticians until the 1950s.

The building remains little changed and now houses the HSBC Bank (formerly the Midland Bank).

Around & About

Opening ceremony for the park fountain, 31 October 1907. The fountain was declared operational by the Mayor and Corporation on the same day that the new Station Road extension and North Town School were opened. Refurbishment work was due to start on the fountain and the park grounds late in 2000.

Turnpike House, Halcon Corner, *c.* 1925. The original building was situated just west of Halcon Corner but was then demolished in 1929 and erected as a private house about 100 yards to the north-east.

Although bypassed by Toneway for through traffic, Halcon Corner is still a busy road. The former Ilminster Road, now closed at the motorway junction, gives access to modern housing estates at Blackbrook. Traffic lights were erected here early in 2000.

Mansfield Road, *c.* 1910. The road first appears on a town map dated 1903 but the houses (nos. 1–29) are not listed in a directory until 1906. Building in the street would appear to have been completed between these two dates.

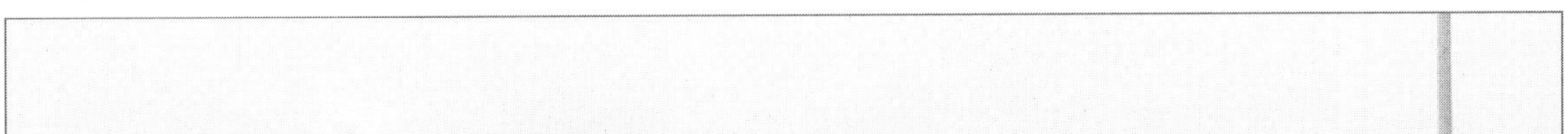

Originally Mansfield Road was an important link between Billetfield and Silver Street. After the completion of Hurdle Way, the road was converted to west traffic only. St George's Church can be seen behind the trees.

On the Tone, *c.* 1910. This view taken from the footbridge at Tangier shows the Tangier Brewery. This business was started around 1855 by William Ellis Oram formerly landlord of the Four Alls. For a short while, W.E. Oram was in partnership with a Mr Hewett but by 1859 the company was known as W.E. Oram and Sons. When W.E. Oram died in 1860 his sons formed Oram and Co. Tangier Family Brewery. The business was sold to a Captain J. Hoskyn in 1879 and for a couple of years he traded as the Tangier Brewery Co. The brewery closed around 1883. One of the Oram brothers, George, owned the Mary Street Brewery between 1870 and 1879. Oram Company bottles are highly prized by collectors today.

The same view today. The mill stream remains but the old brewery buildings have been demolished.

A view on the old Roman Road, *c.* 1905. This trackway started just beyond the end of East Reach at the former Borough boundary and it ran north-east through open countryside.

This view along the course of the old Roman Road shows the area just to the east of Asda. The entire area has now been developed, the modern Roman Road presumably taking its name from the old trackway. As far as is known it has no Roman connections.

Trinity Street, *c.* 1906. The premises in the right foreground is the old dairy at Trinity Terrace. The church still retains the original pinnacles on its tower, but these were later removed.

Trinity Street today, looking very much the same although the school and dairy have gone. At the far end there used to be a public house, The New Inn, which has now closed.

'French Weir', *c.* 1912. French Weir originally Frensweir, was constructed together with the mill stream to power both the fulling and corn mills which stood at Goodland Gardens where the mill stream rejoins the Tone. In the distance can be seen St Johns Church, consecrated in 1863.

The mill stream and pathway remain much the same today, although the view across fields to St Johns has been obscured by trees.

Priory Weir, *c.* 1905. Priory or Obridge Weir was situated 50 yards east of Obridge Lock. The weir was designed to discharge overflow water from the stream, which served Obridge Mill. The town's sewage works was later built on the site of the mill and the weir served the turbine associated with the works. The lock was demolished in 1980.

After demolition of the lock and weir, Priory Bridge road was reconstructed through the area. Sadly another picturesque area at the edge of the town disappeared under tarmac.

Priory Fields, c. 1905. This view looks west towards the town with the river Tone on the right. This area takes its name from the Augustinian Priory formed in the twelfth century and later dissolved by Henry VIII. Originally the Priory land was bounded by the Borough and St Margaret's leper hospital to the west, by East Reach to the south, and by the river Tone to the north.

All of the former Priory lands have now been built over and the section of river seen above has been filled in. A short road behind the warehouses is still called Priory Fields.

Park Street, *c.* 1905. The street was constructed in 1848 and this photograph was taken from the field in which County Hall was built in 1935. The large building served as the Convent of Perpetual Adoration from 1867 and was purchased by Taunton Corporation in 1929.

Park Street with Debenham's offices on the left. The former convent building is now known as St Paul's House.

A charming view of Burton Place taken from the corner of Wilton Grove. This photo was taken on 14 April 1905 on a dull day with a camera setting of f32 at 1.5 seconds. In the background is Wilton Prison while to the right are Westbourne Cottages.

After the demolition of Westbourne Cottages, new police houses were built in 1915. Much of the former Wilton Prison has also been demolished.

Kingston Road, *c.* 1912. The single decker tram is standing near the passing loop at St Andrew's Road. This section of the tramway system, from the original terminus at the railway station to a new one at the junction of Kingston Road and Salisbury Street, opened on 13 August 1909.

Kingston Road today. St Andrew's Church stands out at the top of the road. The gabled building, centre, served as a Congregational schoolroom for many years.

The Villages

District Nurses at Halse, 1911. Seated is Janet Cross the local nurse who resigned in March 1911. Behind her stands her replacement Nurse Woodland who was approved in May 1911. The new nurse looks very businesslike with her crisp uniform and shiny leather bag.

Bathpool, *c.* 1920. In the middle distance can be seen St Quintin House whilst on the right is the Bathpool Inn.

St Quintin House has now been replaced by the modern St Quintin Park housing estate. The large tree formerly next to the house gates still remains.

Norton Fitzwarren, *c.* 1905. The lane on the right leads to Norton Brewery owned at this time by S.W. Arnold and Sons. On the left is Bay House with the post office behind the boy second from the left. The thatched cottages, centre, have been demolished.

As yet Norton Fitzwarren has no bypass and this section of road is often very busy, quite a contrast from the quiet scene above. Brewery Lane, right, leads to a small trading estate adjacent to the village school.

Norton Fitzwarren, *c.* 1906. The building on the left is the Ring of Bells. The pretty thatched cottages were known as Rose Cottages.

Modern day Norton Fitzwarren certainly lacks the charm it had in the early 1900s. Currently there is talk of a bypass and massive residential development to the south of the village.

Norton Fitzwarren, *c.* 1920. This view shows the exit of the brewery lane from the west. The large flower urn in the garden of Laburnum Cottage can still be seen today although it has been moved a little further from the road.

The thatched cottages in the earlier view have been demolished. The House named 'Loxley' in the centre still remains.

Ford Farm, Norton Fitzwarren, *c.* 1904. Originally there were many thatched buildings in the village, but none now remain. The farmhouse has been completely demolished and the area redeveloped for housing. The farm took its name from the former ford through the river. A bridge can be seen in the middle distance.

The same view in 1999, although the camera angle has been changed slightly to show cars ploughing through floods just before the railway bridge.

Galmington looking towards Trull Road, 1947. At this time the route to Trull Road went via Hoveland Lane until the river was met at Ramshorn Bridge. Road vehicles had then to follow the stream until reaching the continuation of the lane. Even as late as 1947, Galmington still had some semblance of its original hamlet status.

Since 1947 numerous housing estates have been built around Galmington. Galmington Road now bypasses part of Hoveland Lane and occupies the original route of Hoveland Lane beyond Galmington Stream.

Members of the Govier family at Blagdon Hill Chapel, *c.* 1900. Abel and William Govier were farmers and quarry owners in the Blagdon area. The Chapel was built in 1878 and used by a Society of Protestant Dissenting Christians known as the Taunton Village Evangelistic Society.

Melody Cottage, the former Blagdon Hill Chapel. The chapel was sold in 1954 for £285 and converted into a cottage. In 2000 the cottage 'with breath taking views' was up for sale for £160,000.

Windmill Hill, North Curry, *c.* 1910. The Wesleyan Chapel on the right was built in 1833.

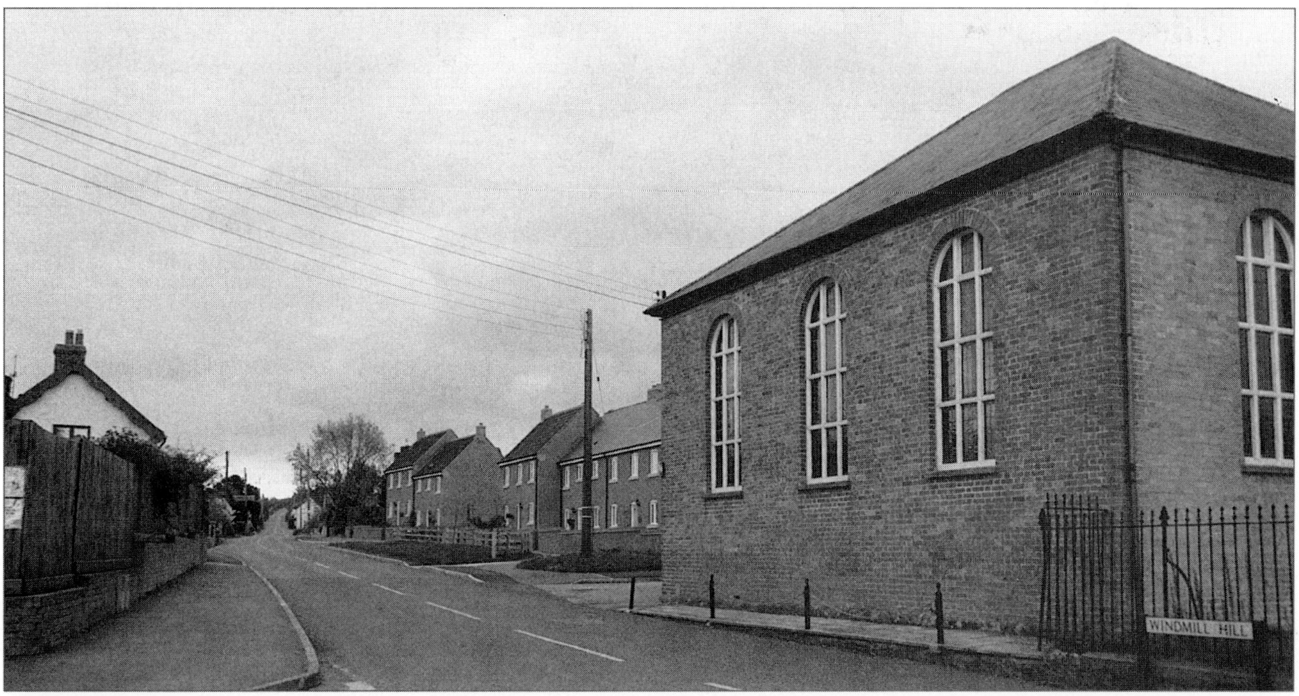

Windmill Hill in 1999, is very modern in appearance but lacks the charm of the older view. New houses have been built beyond the chapel.

Greggs Hill and Post Office, Stoke St Gregory, *c.* 1910. The Chapel House is visible in the distance. To the left is the entrance to the Baptist Church.

The cottage on the right no longer houses the post office as it has moved further up the road.

Hatch Beachamp Post Office, *c.* 1910. An earlier view of the post office shows it situated next to the Hatch Inn.

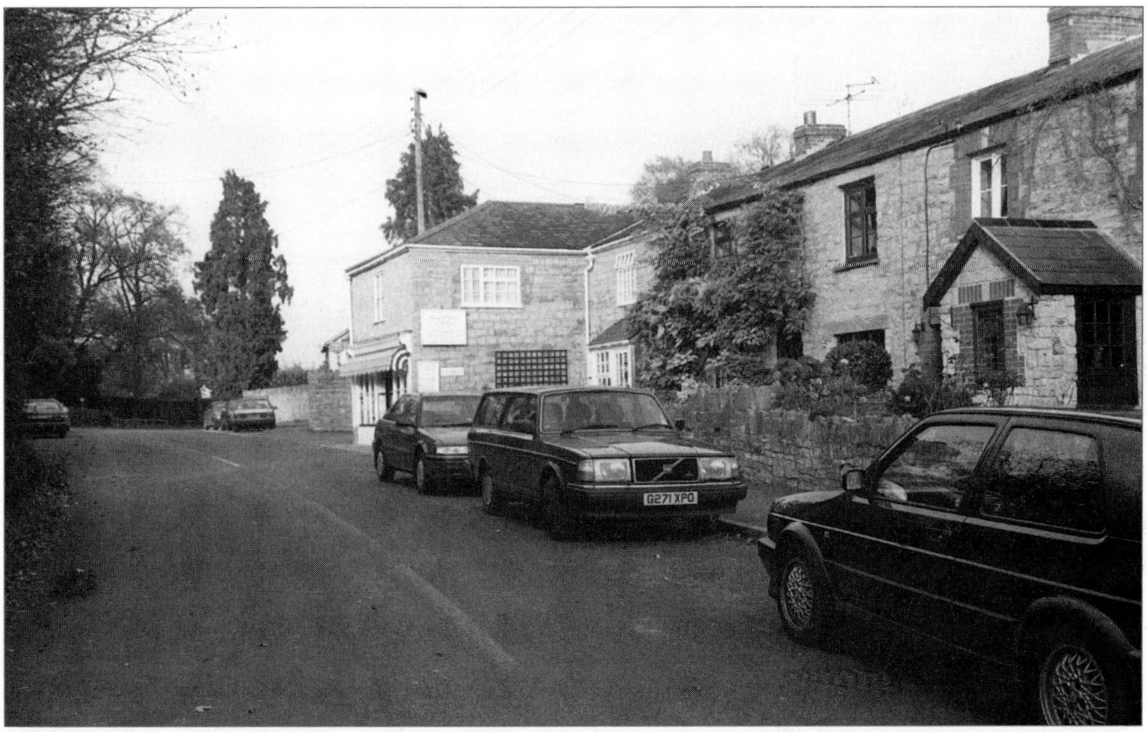

The post office remains much the same, although the buildings pictured beyond it in the photograph above have been removed. At a time of great change in cash handling and communications, the rural post office is increasingly coming under threat of closure.

Hatch Station, *c.* 1910 taken by local photographer J.F. Bridel. This view shows the portal of the 154-yard-long Hatch Tunnel. The 13-mile branch line was opened in 1866 and ran from Creech Junction to Chard. The signal rodding on the right leads from the signal box which is just out of view.

A sorry sight for railway enthusiasts! The little brick station building still remains but is falling into disrepair. The line closed in 1964 and the station is now used for industrial purposes.

Wrantage Post Office, *c.* 1908. This is a splendid view of Mr Goss outside his post office and shop. The placards are interesting as one suggests a date for the photograph. The reference to Turkey probably dates to 1908 when the Young Turk Party took power, ultimately deposing the Sultan in 1909. Mr Goss was also deacon and treasurer of Hatch Baptist Chapel.

A sad sign of the times. Wrantage Post Office vacant and for sale in 1999, the last sub postmistress, Mrs Robertson, having recently closed the business.

East Lyng Garage, *c.* 1930. This is a lovely advertising postcard for Ames and Sons garage. The car in the centre is a Rover registered to Mr G.M. Duke of Ruishton, 8 July 1926.

There is still a garage and filling station at Lyng some seventy years later. The premises have been rebuilt and the forecourt expanded. The author's Rover, left, has much evolved from its predecessor in the older view.

York Inn, Churchinford, *c.* 1920. Years ago the village inn used to be the social centre of a small community. Now they are declining at a rate of six per week. Few are able to sustain a viable business without casting their customer base a lot wider and a good food menu is almost a necessity. Public houses lost locally in the last 10 years include the Wheelwrights Arms at Wrantage, The Crown at West Buckland, The Stags Head at Seven Ash, The Royal Oak at Wiveliscombe and the Gardeners Arms at Bishops Lydeard.

The thatched portion of the inn has been converted to tiles in common with many such properties in rural areas over the last seventy years.

Park Cycle Depot at no. 48 Upper High Street, *c.* 1910. This shop was situated just beyond the Temple Methodist Church going towards High Street. The business was established by Charles Lock around 1905. Mr Lock also owned the Borough Cycle Works in Corporation Street.

Acknowledgements & Picture Credits

The author would like to thank the following for help in compiling this book: Phil Perryman, Taunton Camera Centre, David Bromwich at the Local Studies Library, Mrs Robertson late of Wrantage Post Office, Mrs M.K. Blackmore, Andy Criddle, Tony Norris, Ken and Peter Talbot, Mrs Kathleen Hill, Keith Thompson, Peter Johnson, Iris Williams, Steve and Janet Pike, Peter Salter (PCS) and Vicky Chipchase.

All photographs are the author's. The following publishers produced the top photographs on pages: W. & E. Bailey 63, 117, 109; Baker (Taunton) half title page, 12, 17; Boots Ltd 14, 100; Brice (Taunton) 47, 101; Buchanen 72, 75; Burrow (Cheltenham) 13; H.C. Colman (Taunton) 29; H.M. Cooper 45; E.E. Cox (Taunton) 33; Frith 23, 25, 55, 99; T. Giblett (North Curry) 113; E.H.C. Gill (Taunton) 43; Lillywhite 18, 36; Miers Series 119; Montague Cooper 95, 98, 102; National Series 104; Photo and Fine Art Co. 97; Senior & Co. 96; Talbot Collection 74; Valentine 22.

If readers can supply additional information or lend original photographs for copying, I hope they will contact me at: 36 Scafell Close, Taunton, Somerset, TA1 4LG.

Marshalsea's Napier bus at an unknown location, *c.* 1920.